Teach

Narnia

Barnabas
in
Schools

Barnabas for Children® is a registered word mark and the logo is a registered device mark of
The Bible Reading Fellowship.
Text copyright © Olivia Warburton 2013
Illustrations copyright © Colin Howard 2013
The author asserts the moral right
to be identified as the author of this work

Published by
The Bible Reading Fellowship
15 The Chambers, Vineyard
Abingdon OX14 3FE
United Kingdom
Tel: +44 (0)1865 319700
Email: enquiries@brf.org.uk
Website: www.brf.org.uk
BRF is a Registered Charity

ISBN 978 0 85746 256 5

First published 2013
10 9 8 7 6 5 4 3 2 1 0
All rights reserved

Acknowledgments

Unless otherwise stated, scripture quotations are taken from the Contemporary English
Version of the Bible published by HarperCollins Publishers, copyright © 1991, 1992, 1995
American Bible Society.

Scripture quotations taken from the Holy Bible, New International Version, copyright © 1973,
1978, 1984 by International Bible Society, are used by permission of Hodder & Stoughton
Publishers, a member of the Hachette Livre Group UK. All rights reserved. 'NIV' is a registered
trademark of International Bible Society. UK trademark number 1448790.

The paper used in the production of this publication was supplied by mills that source their
raw materials from sustainably managed forests. Soy-based inks were used in its printing and
the laminate film is biodegradable.

A catalogue record for this book is available from the British Library

Printed in Singapore by Craft Print International Ltd

Teaching
Narnia

A cross-curricular classroom
and assembly resource for RE teachers

Olivia Warburton

~ Acknowledgments ~

Many thanks to Sarah Gibbs, Chris Hudson, Louisa Lapworth,
Katharina Walls, Michael Ward and Karen Wymbs for their
invaluable comments and suggestions.

Contents

Foreword

The Chronicles of Narnia are so rich in invention and so deep in spiritual and moral content that they lend themselves ideally for use in school. Themes of friendship, perception, identity, forgiveness and many others abound throughout 'The Narniad' (as it has been called), and can be most usefully turned to educational effect both in the context of assemblies and in RE courses.

Of course, using the Narnia books in the classroom in order to teach children lessons was not the primary function Lewis had in mind for the Chronicles when he published them in the 1950s. His main aim was simply to tell seven enjoyable stories that would appeal to the imagination. Lewis was, above all things, a poet—that is to say, a 'maker', a literary man who valued the imaginative exercise of immersing oneself in a sub-created world, even if one didn't always like or agree with everything that one found there.

In *An Experiment in Criticism*, Lewis draws a distinction between 'using' and 'receiving' literature. To 'receive' a story is simply to follow its guiding hand, allowing oneself to be led through a pattern or dance of imaginative activities which are good for their own sake. To 'use' a story is to draw out principles or lessons from that pattern, putting the story in service of some aim or objective that one brings to the story.

Religious education is one such aim that can be brought to the Narnia septet and Olivia Warburton has done an excellent job of using the Chronicles in a way which goes with their grain. The lesson plans to be found in *Teaching Narnia* use Lewis's stories in a sensitive and intelligent fashion and skilfully avoid reducing these classic tales to a mere quarry for moral or religious pedagogy. After the points have been made and the lessons taught (and hopefully learnt!), the stories still stand as just that—stories that are to be received freely on their own terms, working whatever degree of magic they can enthral us with, inspiring, frightening, exciting, moving us, leading us through a satisfying dance of the imagination, which needs no further justification—the hallmark of all great narrative art.

Dr Michael Ward, University of Oxford
Coeditor, *The Cambridge Companion to C.S. Lewis*

Introduction

Teaching Narnia draws on C.S. Lewis's classic series, 'The Chronicles of Narnia', to provide classroom and assembly material for Primary RE teachers. The seven stories that make up the Chronicles were originally published in London between October 1950 and March 1956. They have been adapted for radio, theatre, television and film, selling over 100 million copies in 47 languages.

Why teach Narnia in RE?

C.S. Lewis was a Christian writer, and the Narnia books, while being presented as fantasy stories, contain strong Christian themes, exploring the nature of Christianity and God's relationship with human beings in a parallel universe. People debate how 'evangelistic' Lewis was intending to be when he wrote the stories. He claimed that the idea for *The Lion, the Witch and the Wardrobe* came from a picture in his head, and that the Christian elements were a byproduct of who he was as a Christian. That is, he naturally wrote about the things he believed in and felt were important.

In his essay 'Sometimes fairy stories may say best what's to be said' (*Of Other Worlds: Essays and Stories*), Lewis wrote:

Some people seem to think that I began by asking myself how I could say something about Christianity to children; then fixed on the fairy tale as an instrument; then collected information about child-psychology and decided what age group I'd write for; then drew up a list of basic Christian truths and hammered out 'allegories' to embody them. This is all pure moonshine.

He explains:

Everything began with images; a faun carrying an umbrella, a queen on a sledge, a magnificent lion. At first there wasn't anything Christian about them; that element pushed itself in of its own accord.

Unlike the Harry Potter books, for example, the series developed book by book rather than being planned from the start, so when Lewis wrote *The Lion, the Witch and the Wardrobe* he didn't know it would be the first—and most famous—of a series of seven.

It seems that he also wrote the stories to work on different levels. Many people read and enjoy the stories without noticing the Christian themes and symbols. They are exciting adventures in their own right, and Christianity is certainly not the only influence. Lewis includes characters from Greek and Roman mythology as well as traditional British and Irish fairy tales, and even Father Christmas makes an appearance.

For others, the Christian element adds a layer of meaning. This makes the stories an ideal focus for RE teaching. They offer parallels with the Bible and the life of Jesus Christ, helping children to learn *about* key Christian beliefs and to learn *from* them by tackling big questions such as: What is really real? How do we see the world? Who is in charge of the world? Is God really good? Does he exist at all? What happens after death? How do we know what is right and wrong?

The stories also provide strong links to PSHE and Citizenship, exploring values and offering life lessons about how we, as individuals, react and respond in different situations.

Finally, the stories promote learning in other curriculum areas such as Literacy, Art, Drama and Science, offer opportunities to develop critical thinking skills and, last but not least, encourage reading for enjoyment.

But what about...?

Over the years certain criticisms have been made of the Narnia stories. These are briefly listed below, since they may be raised in class discussion or you may have wondered about them yourself. For a more detailed analysis, see the helpful articles at www.narniaweb.com/resources-links/are-the-chronicles-of-narnia-sexist-and-racist and www.michaelward.net/writing/articles.

Objection 1: Lewis's attitude to gender

There are certain points in the stories where girls are treated differently from boys. For example, Susan and Lucy are not allowed to fight in the battle at the end of *The Lion, the Witch and the Wardrobe*, but Peter and Edmund are.

- **Remember** that C.S. Lewis was writing in the 1950s, and his writing reflected the attitudes of his time concerning the roles of men and women.
- **Note** that many of the girls in Narnia are very strong characters —Polly, Lucy, Aravis, Jill—who are often right when the boys are wrong.
- **Consider** that Lucy has an especially close relationship with Aslan, and that she and Susan are the only ones to witness his death; **compare** with the faithful women followers of Jesus going to the tomb, and Mary Magdalene being the first to see the risen Christ (see the Bible account in John 20:11–18).

Objection 2: Lewis's attitude to sexuality

Susan does not enter Aslan's Country at the end of *The Last Battle*. This seems to be linked with her interest in 'nylons and lipstick and invitations' (LB, ch. 12).

- **Note** that Susan's physical attractiveness is presented positively in *The Horse and His Boy*.
- **Remember** that the last book in the series (and one of C.S. Lewis's own letters) does leave open the possibility that Susan will return to Narnia/Aslan's Country in the end.
- **Consider** that other characters feel that Susan wants to grow up too fast; **compare** with the current debate about the sexualisation of young girls.

Objection 3: Racial and religious prejudice

The Calormenes, who have a different skin colour and religion from the Narnians (they worship the god Tash), are generally portrayed negatively.

- **Note** that this kind of stereotyping is not uncommon in children's literature, where 'baddies' often have few redeeming features, and that C.S. Lewis was writing in the days before political correctness.
- **Remember** that there are good Calormenes, such as Aravis, the heroine of *The Horse and His Boy*, and Emeth, the brave young soldier in *The Last Battle*.
- **Consider** that Lewis seems to want to discourage the reader from jumping to conclusions about anyone's ultimate fate. There are a few unexpected arrivals in Aslan's Country, and more than once Aslan discourages speculation by one character about another, saying, 'That is their story, not yours.'

How to use this book

Teaching Narnia contains 15 lesson plans for use in the classroom, a drama workshop and two themed outlines for collective worship, together with follow-up ideas for 'Thought for the Day'. Each lesson plan contains the following elements:

- Learning objectives
- Cross-curricular links
- Starter
- Classroom activities
- Extension activities where appropriate
- Our Bible link: the Contemporary English Version is used, but other versions can be found at www.biblegateway.com. In most cases these passages are intended to be used to provide a moment of reflection at the end of the lesson, leading into the reflective corner, but in some lessons they are integrated with specific activities.
- Reflective corner

Each lesson plan contains at least 30–40 minutes' worth of teaching material. This can be abbreviated or combined with another session, depending on the time available. The first lesson, 'Starting out with C.S. Lewis', provides an essential introduction to the topic, and 'Mended world' follows on from 'Spoiled world'. Other lessons can be taken in any order or omitted altogether if not required.

Age range/differentiation

Children aged between eight and twelve years are the primary readership for the Narnia stories, so the material in this book is designed primarily for Key Stage 2. Certain activities have been marked as being suitable also for Foundation Stage and/or Key Stage 1, as even very young children can discuss good and evil and relate to certain characters and situations. Look for the icons:

Plot summaries

Some people—both teachers and children—will already be familiar with the stories; for those who are not, the plot summaries at the end of this resource will provide helpful background. The classroom activities use extracts from the books and clips from the films, so no prior knowledge is assumed.

Use of other media

Several of the activities suggest playing a short clip from one of the Walden Media films. If this is not possible, an extract from the relevant book can be read out instead.

Support materials

The six worksheets are available to download in A4 format at www.barnabasinschools.org.uk/extra-resources/, and all web links cited in the book are listed on a single page in the same download file for easy reference.

Lesson plans

Lesson plan:
Starting out with C.S. Lewis

Learning objectives

- To learn about C.S. Lewis's life and its historical context
- To explore how events in our lives may influence us
- To start to think about how we respond to these events

Cross-curricular links

History, PSHE, Literacy

Starter

Play brief soundbites of some well-known film theme tunes (for example, *Star Wars*, *The Lord of the Rings*, *Harry Potter*) and ask the class to identify them. Include the theme tune for the Walden Media film *The Lion, the Witch and the Wardrobe*. You can find this on the CD of the official soundtrack or on the internet.

Activity: Step back in time

Show the class a picture of C.S. Lewis (for example, the photograph from his Wikipedia entry at http://en.wikipedia.org/wiki/C._S._Lewis) and ask them to say how long ago they think this man lived, judging by the style of the photo and what he is wearing.

Now let's get historical with a quick quiz:

- **1898 or 1963?** British pop group The Beatles release their first two albums. *[1963]*

- **1898 or 1963?** Enzo Ferrari, racing car driver and manufacturer, is born. *[1898]*
- **1898 or 1963?** Caleb Bradham names his soft drink Pepsi-Cola. *[1898]*
- **1898 or 1963?** *Dr No*, the first James Bond film, is shown in American cinemas. *[1963]*

C.S. Lewis, the author of the Narnia series, was born in 1898 and died in 1963. We're going to find out some more facts about him.

Hand out the worksheet on page 19 and ask the class to identify the happy and sad events in C.S. Lewis's life, either by highlighting the words in the text or by marking up the timeline. Alternatively, you could read out the text and ask the class to call out when something happy or sad happens. You may wish to include 'depends' as a third option to allow more room for interpretation.

Pick out the word 'reluctantly', explaining it if necessary, and ask the class whether they think that means Lewis was happy or sad—or both—about becoming a Christian. Can they identify with the feeling of doing something you believe is right when it isn't what you really want to do?

Activity: Into the mind of the author

Play the video clip 'The Lion Awakes' about C.S. Lewis's early life, from the internet. From watching this clip and from what you have just learnt about Lewis's life, can you guess what might be some of the important themes in the Narnia stories?

Our Bible link: Psalm 139:7–12

C.S. Lewis felt that he could not escape from God. The person who wrote this psalm hundreds of years ago says the same thing, and, again like Lewis, it is not entirely clear whether he is happy or sad about this.

Where could I go to escape
from your Spirit or from your sight?
If I were to climb up to the highest heavens,
you would be there.
If I were to dig down to the world of the dead
you would also be there.

Suppose I had wings like the dawning day
and flew across the ocean.
Even then your powerful arm
would guide and protect me.
Or suppose I said, 'I'll hide in the dark
until night comes to cover me over.'
But you see in the dark
because daylight and dark are all the same to you.

Reflective corner

Props needed: A poster, mug or T-shirt with the slogan 'Keep Calm and Carry On'

Think about how sad things happened in C.S. Lewis's life, and yet reading his stories has made many people very happy. How have other people helped you when you were feeling sad? What helps you to 'keep calm and carry on'? How could you encourage others to 'keep calm and carry on'?

- See 'Beautiful world', 'Spoiled world' and 'Mended world' for more on key themes within the Narnia stories.
- 'Dealing with feelings' provides further material on how C.S. Lewis's experiences may have influenced the stories he wrote.

Worksheet: The life of C.S. Lewis

Background

Clive Staples Lewis was born in Belfast on 29 November 1898. His childhood was happy until his mother died of cancer in 1908, when he was nine years old. He was then sent away to boarding school. In 1916 he won a scholarship to University College, Oxford, but left in 1917 to fight in World War I, arriving on his 19th birthday. He was wounded and returned to his studies in 1918 when the war ended. He went on to teach philosophy and medieval literature to university students.

He became a Christian, very reluctantly, in his early 30s, and from that point on put a lot of effort into debating with people of different views and writing books about the Christian faith. He then wrote the Narnia stories, published between 1950 and 1956. He married Joy Davidman Gresham in 1956, but she died of cancer four years later. C.S. Lewis died on 22 November 1963.

Timeline

1898: C.S. Lewis is born
1908: Lewis's mother dies
1908: Lewis is sent to boarding school
1914: World War I begins
1916: Lewis goes to university
1917: Lewis goes to fight in the war
1918: Lewis is wounded
1918: World War I ends
1918: Lewis returns to university
1931: Lewis becomes a Christian
1939: World War II starts
1945: World War II ends
1950–56: The Narnia books are published
1956: Lewis marries Joy Davidman Gresham
1960: Lewis's wife dies
1963: C.S. Lewis dies

Lesson plan: Out of this world

Learning objectives

- To engage imaginatively with the concept of different worlds
- To reflect on what our own world is like
- To connect the world of Narnia with the idea of heaven

Cross-curricular links

Literacy, Art, Citizenship, Science

Starter FS KS1

Have you ever been to another country? Was it just the same as here, or different?

Alternatively, what stories have you read about other worlds? Do they have anything in common? (For example: magic, different laws of space and time, talking animals, monsters...)

Activity: Spot the difference KS1

Read the following passages from *The Voyage of the Dawn Treader*, which describe how the world of Narnia is different from ours.

'Narnian time flows differently from ours. If you spent a hundred years in Narnia, you would still come back to our world at the very same hour of the very same day on which you left. And then, if you went back to Narnia

after spending a week here, you might find that a thousand Narnian years had passed, or only a day, or no time at all. You never know till you get there.' (VDT, ch. 1)

'Do you mean to say,' asked Caspian, 'that you three come from a round world (round like a ball) and you've never told me! It's really too bad of you. Because we have fairy-tales in which there are round worlds and I always loved them. I never believed there were any real ones… Have you ever been to the parts where people walk about upside-down?'

Edmund shook his head. 'And it isn't like that,' he added. 'There's nothing particularly exciting about a round world when you're there.' (VDT, ch. 15)

In groups, look at the map of Narnia: www.thenarniaacademy.org/large_map.htm. Create your own world and draw a map of it, giving it a name and labelling cities, mountains, rivers, forests and deserts (if it has any of these things). In your group or with a partner, think about how and why your imaginary world is different from ours.

Read your descriptions to the rest of the class (perhaps in the style of a travel brochure, trying to persuade them to visit), who could score each world according to criteria such as scenery, danger, weather, food and so on.

Activity: A door from the world of men

'A door from the world of men! I have heard of such things.' (LWW, ch. 4)

In *The Lion, the Witch and the Wardrobe*, Lucy hides in a wardrobe… and finds herself in a snowy wood. You might like to play the sequence from the film (Scene 3, from 10:50 to 13:15).

She took a step further in—then two or three steps—always expecting to feel woodwork against the tips of her fingers. But she could not feel it.

'This must be a simply enormous wardrobe!' thought Lucy, going

21

still further in and pushing the soft folds of the coats aside to make room for her...

A moment later she found that she was standing in the middle of a wood at night-time with snow under her feet and snowflakes falling through the air. (LWW, ch. 1)

Let's take a look at how other characters move in and out of Narnia.

In *The Magician's Nephew*, Polly and Digory use magic green and yellow rings. They also jump into different pools in the Wood between the Worlds to get to different worlds.

In *Prince Caspian*, the children are dragged off a station platform by the sound of Susan's magical horn and find themselves 'standing in a woody place' (PC, ch. 1). They return home through a wooden door standing by itself with nothing around it. This wooden door frame reappears in *The Last Battle*.

In *The Voyage of the Dawn Treader*, Lucy, Edmund and Eustace are sucked into a picture on the bedroom wall and end up in the middle of the Narnian sea.

In *The Silver Chair*, Jill and Eustace open a disused door in the wall of the school grounds:

They had expected to see the grey, heathery slope of the moor going up and up to join the dull autumn sky. Instead, a blaze of sunshine met them... And the sunlight was coming from what certainly did look like a different world.' (SC, ch. 1)

How would you feel, arriving suddenly in a new world? Draw a big empty door frame on a piece of paper and write all the adjectives you can think of inside it.

Which of these different 'portals' do you think is most exciting?

Write a short description of a different way of getting to another world. You could storyboard it as follows:

- I would get to another world by...
- I think this would be...
- To help me, I would need...

Extension activity

Scientists talk about 'multiverses'. Find out what these are. The Super Mario Multiverse video on www.popsci.com gives an accessible introduction.

Our Bible link: Luke 18:15–17

Christians believe that heaven is a reality, not a made-up place or a fantasy, and that Jesus is the way into this 'other world', the kingdom of heaven. According to Jesus, children were well placed to find out more about it.

Some people brought their little children for Jesus to bless. But when his disciples saw them doing this, they told the people to stop bothering him. So Jesus called the children over to him and said, 'Let the children come to me! Don't try to stop them. People who are like these children belong to God's kingdom. You will never get into God's kingdom unless you enter it like a child!'

Reflective corner

Props needed: A globe; two large posters, one saying THANK YOU and the other PLEASE

Ask the children to draw or write one thing they like about the world and one thing they would like to change. They can stick their work on to the posters, possibly while music is playing.

⁂

Lesson plan:
Seeing things differently

Learning objectives

- To be willing to question assumptions about what is real
- To be open to new ideas and able to see other points of view
- To express what we believe to be true and important

Cross-curricular links

Literacy, PSHE

Starter

Sit in a circle and play a quick game where each child has to complete the sentence 'In my new world…' The more imaginative the answers, the better! This could be turned into a memory game by asking children to repeat the previous answers as well as their own.

Activity: Now you see it, now you don't

Show a photograph of the statue in Belfast of C.S. Lewis looking into the wardrobe. (Go to C.S. Lewis's Wikipedia entry and scroll down.)

Hand out copies of the worksheet on page 27 and ask the class if the poem makes sense. Could the writer really have seen these things?

Then ask them to draw forward slashes as follows, so that each line 'reads over' to the next: 'I saw a peacock / With a fiery tail I saw a blazing comet / Drop down hail I saw a cloud,' and so on.

I saw a peacock / with a fiery tail
I saw a blazing comet / drop down hail
I saw a cloud / with ivy circled round
I saw a sturdy oak / creep on the ground
I saw an ant / swallow up a whale
I saw a raging sea / brim full of ale
I saw a Venice glass / sixteen foot deep
I saw a well / full of men's tears that weep
I saw their eyes / all in a flame of fire
I saw a house / as big as the moon and higher
I saw the sun / even in the midst of night
I saw the man that saw this wondrous sight.

Ask the class if the poem makes better sense now. Has the impossible become possible?

Activity: What is really real?

Sometimes C.S. Lewis told his brother stories as they sat among the coats in their grandfather's old wardrobe. The wardrobe is now kept at Wheaton College in America, with a sign on it saying: 'Enter at your own risk. The Wade Center assumes no responsibility for persons who disappear or who are lost in this wardrobe.'

In *The Lion, the Witch and the Wardrobe*, Peter says to the Professor:

'If things are real, they're there all the time.'
'Are they?' said the Professor...
'But do you really mean, sir,' said Peter, 'that there could be other worlds—all over the place, just round the corner—like that?'
'Nothing is more probable,' said the Professor. (LWW, ch. 5)

Roleplay: Spend five minutes in pairs, one person being the Professor (giving reasons why other worlds could exist) and the other being Peter (giving reasons why they couldn't). You might want to write your arguments down first.

Alternatively: In *The Silver Chair*, the Green Witch pretends that there is no Narnia, that it is 'all a dream', and Jill, Eustace and Puddleglum try to describe it to her. How would you convince someone who didn't believe in our world that it was real? Working with a partner, create a list of reasons ('Our world is real because…') and share them with the class.

Our Bible link: John 20:24–27

Jesus' friend Thomas didn't like to believe in anything he couldn't see, and he didn't believe the other disciples when they told him that Jesus, who had died on the cross, was alive again.

Although Thomas the Twin was one of the twelve disciples, he wasn't with the others when Jesus appeared to them. So they told him, 'We have seen the Lord!'

But Thomas said, 'First, I must see the nail scars in his hands and touch them with my finger. I must put my hand where the spear went into his side. I won't believe unless I do this!'

A week later the disciples were together again. This time, Thomas was with them. Jesus came in while the doors were still locked and stood in the middle of the group. He greeted his disciples and said to Thomas, 'Put your finger here and look at my hands! Put your hand into my side. Stop doubting and have faith!'

Reflective corner

Props needed: A hologram or kaleidoscope

Why might it sometimes be helpful to look at situations differently? How easy do you find it to see another point of view?

Worksheet: Now you see it, now you don't

I saw a peacock with a fiery tail
I saw a blazing comet drop down hail
I saw a cloud with ivy circled round
I saw a sturdy oak creep on the ground
I saw an ant swallow up a whale
I saw a raging sea brim full of ale
I saw a Venice glass sixteen foot deep
I saw a well full of men's tears that weep
I saw their eyes all in a flame of fire
I saw a house as big as the moon and higher
I saw the sun even in the midst of night
I saw the man that saw this wondrous sight.

ANON, 17TH CENTURY

Lesson plan:
Dealing with feelings

Learning objectives

- To explore possible reasons for writing about a different world
- To think about how we deal with difficult emotions
- To understand that we are not alone in feeling this way

Cross-curricular links

History, PSHE, Literacy, Art

Starter

Play some video footage of World War II from the internet. You will need to judge what your class can cope with, as some of the content may prove upsetting.

Activity: Why make up another world?

No doubt C.S. Lewis created Narnia partly because he was interested in seeing things differently (see the previous lesson plan). Let's look at some other possible reasons why a person might want to imagine a different world.

Reason 1: To express feelings and ask questions

Many of the sad events in C.S. Lewis' life are echoed in the Narnia stories.

- Digory's mother is dying of cancer in *The Magician's Nephew*.
- The Pevensie children are sent away from home during the war, and Jill and Eustace are unhappy at their boarding school.
- C.S. Lewis lived through two World Wars, and there is a great deal of fighting in the Narnia series.

Discuss: What helps you to express your feelings? Would you put your feelings into a story or poem? Why, or why not?

Reason 2: To escape from the world you're in

Creating a magical land where miracles can happen is a way of 'rewriting' real life for both author and readers.

- The Narnia stories were written in the years following World War II. For many English children in 1950, life was tough. Many would have lost friends and family in the war. Food and clothing were scarce.
- In Narnia, Digory is given a magical apple that heals his dying mother. This didn't happen for Lewis's own mother.
- Jill and Eustace escape to Narnia from the school they hate and the people who are bullying them—not normally an option.

Discuss: If you are finding something hard, do you think it can help to forget about it for a while? Can you think of some helpful ways of doing this?

Activity: Sharing in the sadness

Working in groups, copy out the Bible passage on page 30 (Psalm 137:1–3) and annotate it with pictures or symbols to explore its meaning. If working on the computer, children could access a safe clipart website to copy and paste appropriate images.

Extension activity

Children could use the internet to find images of Babylon and Jerusalem and research what these sixth-century BC Jews might have looked like.

Our Bible link: Psalm 137:1–3

In 586BC the people of Jerusalem had to leave their homes when the king of Babylonia (modern-day Iraq) conquered the city and took them back to Babylon. This psalm expresses their feelings.

Beside the rivers of Babylon we thought about Jerusalem,
and we sat down and cried.
We hung our small harps on the willow trees.
Our enemies had brought us here as their prisoners,
and now they wanted us to sing and entertain them.
They insulted us and shouted, 'Sing about Zion!'

Reflective corner

Props needed: Paper and pens

Are there any sad feelings that you would like to express through words or pictures, or something you would like to 'rewrite'?

Lesson plan: Making everything better

Learning objectives

- To explore the concept of heaven and what it represents
- To critically assess music, artwork and literature on this theme
- To compare C.S. Lewis's idea of heaven with other people's perspectives

Cross-curricular links

Music, Art, Literacy, PSHE

Starter

Ask the class to say how they think a song about a new world might sound—loud or soft, exciting or mysterious? Then play 'New World' by TobyMac, from the CD *Music Inspired By The Chronicles of Narnia* (2005) or from the internet, which describes Lucy's arrival in Narnia and what happens next. You may wish to print out the lyrics (do an internet search on 'new world tobymac lyrics').

Activity: Heaven in music

In *The Magician's Nephew* C.S. Lewis describes the beginning of Narnia. In *The Last Battle* he shows it coming to an end, and gives a vision of the new Narnia—heaven. Be aware that some children may find a discussion of heaven upsetting—for example, if they have recently suffered a bereavement.

Play one or more of the following songs about heaven (all available on Spotify), and ask the class for their reactions to the music and words:

- 'Tears in heaven' by Eric Clapton: Clapton's five-year-old son died in an accident. This song questions whether they will still recognise each other in heaven.
- 'Will you meet me in heaven?' by Johnny Cash: Cash thinks the answer is definitely yes.
- 'Where the streets have no name' by U2: believe it or not, this is a song about heaven.
- 'This is home' by Switchfoot: this expresses the idea of heaven as home ('after all my searching... after all my questions...').

Activity: Heaven in pictures

Ask the class to share or sketch their ideas about what they think heaven might look like. (Children who say 'I don't believe in heaven' can still be included in this activity if you rephrase it as 'What do you think someone who believes in heaven would imagine it to be like?') Then show them some visual interpretations (Google Images will provide a wide range, some more clichéd than others) and ask whether they think these images come anywhere close to what it might really be like. Why is it so difficult to draw heaven?

Activity: Heaven in words

C.S. Lewis makes several different attempts to describe the heavenly Narnia. Working in pairs, read the extracts on the worksheet (see page 34) and decide which is your favourite description and why. Then write your own short descriptions of what you think heaven could be like and create a classroom wall display.

Give each pair a selection of ripe, unblemished fruit to taste as a way of experiencing the first passage more fully. Sparkling or flavoured water could symbolise the 'sweet' water of the fourth passage.

Our Bible link: Revelation 21:1, 3–4

A long time ago, a man called John received a vision of the future, with all the bad bits taken out.

I saw a new heaven and a new earth. The first heaven and the first earth had disappeared, and so had the sea... I heard a loud voice shout from the throne:

'God's home is now with his people. He will live with them, and they will be his own. Yes, God will make his home among his people. He will wipe all tears from their eyes, and there will be no more death, suffering, crying, or pain. These things of the past are gone for ever.'

Reflective corner

Props needed: Sheets of paper with sentence stems as follows:

- There will be no more DEATH...
- There will be no more SUFFERING...
- There will be no more CRYING...

Each child, working alone or in pairs, should complete a line as follows. For example:

- There will be no more DEATH... because we will live for ever.
- There will be no more SUFFERING... because all pain is gone.
- There will be no more CRYING... because we will be full of joy.

Children could bring their lines together to make a whole-class poem about heaven.

Worksheet: Heaven in words

Extract 1

What was the fruit like? Unfortunately no one can describe a taste. All I can say is that, compared with those fruits, the freshest grapefruit you've ever eaten was dull, and the juiciest orange was dry, and the most melting pear was hard and woody, and the sweetest wild strawberry was sour. (LB, ch. 13)

Extract 2

It was the Unicorn who summed up what everyone was feeling. He stamped his right fore-hoof on the ground and neighed, and then cried:

'I have come home at last! This is my real country! I belong here. This is the land I have been looking for all my life, though I never knew it till now. The reason why we loved the old Narnia is that it sometimes looked a little like this.' (LB, ch. 15)

Extract 3

Lucy says, 'This is still Narnia, and more real and more beautiful than the Narnia down below' (LB, ch. 16).

Extract 4

In *The Voyage of the Dawn Treader*, Reepicheep is looking for Aslan's Country. He has received this promise:

'Where sky and water meet,
Where the waves grow sweet,
Doubt not, Reepicheep,
To find all you seek,
There is the utter East.' (VDT, ch. 2)

Lesson plan:
It all began with a picture

Starter

Discuss the following questions with a partner or in a group: What is your favourite story and why do you like it? What picture comes into your head when you think about it?

Activity: It all began with a picture

Listen to how C.S. Lewis came up with the idea for *The Lion, the Witch and the Wardrobe*. He wrote about it in an essay called 'It all began with a picture':

The Lion *all began with a picture of a Faun carrying an umbrella and parcels in a snowy wood. This picture had been in my mind since I was about sixteen. Then one day, when I was about forty, I said to myself: 'Let's try to make a story about it.'*

He explains:

At first I had very little idea how the story would go. But then suddenly Aslan came bounding into it. I think I had been having a good many dreams of lions about that time. Apart from that, I don't know where the Lion came from or why he came. But once he was there, he pulled the whole story together, and soon he pulled the six other Narnian stories in after him.

Choose one of the following phrases and write a story or poem around it. These are all images from *The Voyage of the Dawn Treader*:

- A dragon crying in a lonely valley
- A golden figure in a pool of water
- A magical book in an empty room
- A dark island where nightmares come true
- Three men in an enchanted sleep

Activity: Showing the story

A book cover needs to communicate visually what the book is about. Design a book cover for one of the Narnia stories, using its title and anything else you know about it to guide you. You can do this with paper and pencils or use PowerPoint.

Alternatively, do an internet search on 'Narnia book cover images'. Which ones do you think communicate the 'meanings' of the books most successfully, and why?

Our Bible link: Genesis 41:17–27

God has a message for the king of Egypt, which he gives through a series of pictures in a dream. But the king needs to find someone to explain to him what the pictures mean.

The king told Joseph:

'I dreamed I was standing on the bank of the River Nile. I saw seven fat, healthy cows come up out of the river, and they began feeding on the grass. Next, seven skinny, bony cows came up out of the river. I have never seen such terrible looking cows anywhere in Egypt. The skinny cows ate the fat ones. But you couldn't tell it, because these skinny cows were just as skinny as they were before. Straight away, I woke up.

'I also dreamed that I saw seven heads of grain growing on one stalk. The heads were full and ripe. Then seven other heads of grain came up. They were thin and scorched by a wind from the desert. These heads of grain swallowed the full ones. I told my dreams to the magicians, but none of them could tell me the meaning of the dreams.'

Joseph replied:

'Your Majesty, both of your dreams mean the same thing, and in them God has shown what he is going to do. The seven good cows stand for seven years, and so do the seven good heads of grain. The seven skinny, ugly cows that came up later also stand for seven years, as do the seven bad heads of grain that were scorched by the east wind. The dreams mean there will be seven years when there won't be enough grain.'

Reflective corner

Props needed: A book and a picture

Words are not the only way to communicate. How can we 'show' respect and concern for each other, for example?

Lesson plan:
Secret messages

Learning objectives

- To understand how stories can have different layers of meaning
- To learn how the medieval view of the planets influenced C.S. Lewis
- To understand that the learning process is ongoing

Cross-curricular links

Literacy, Science, History

Starter

Using dictionaries or an online translation site, find the word for 'lion' in as many languages as you can and create a poster using the different words. What is interesting about the Turkish word? (It is 'Aslan'.)

Activity: Digging deeper

Go to http://kids.niehs.nih.gov/games/illusions/illusion_23.htm. Can you see two elderly faces or a larger scene? Explore some of the other illusions on this website.

There are hidden things to be found in these pictures. The Narnia stories contain many themes and images from the Christian story. They also have a 'hidden' layer discovered by Michael Ward in 2003 and explained in *Planet Narnia* (OUP USA, 2008) and *The Narnia Code* (Paternoster, 2010).

Activity: The secrets of the heavens

Check out the solar system at www.spacekids.co.uk/solarsystem. What we know about it has changed over the centuries. Telescopes were not invented until the early 1600s, so there was a limit to what people could see in the night sky before that time. In medieval times, they could only see seven moving 'stars' in the sky, which have given their names to the days of the week. Can the class work some of these out?

- Monday = Moon-day.
- Tuesday = Mars-day ('mardi' in French).
- Wednesday = Mercury-day ('mercredi' in French).
- Thursday = Jove-day ('jeudi' in French/Thor's-day in Norse). ('Jove' and 'Thor' are alternative names for Jupiter.)
- Friday = Venus-day ('vendredi' in French/Freya-day in Norse). ('Freya' is another name for Venus.)
- Saturday = Saturn-day.
- Sunday = Sun-day.

Look at the worksheet on page 42, comparing what we know now about the solar system with what people thought about the planets in medieval times. What are the differences?

Interesting fact: Pluto was discovered in 1930 and scientists described it as one of the main planets until 2006. Now it is classified as a 'dwarf planet'. We are learning all the time.

The medieval view of the planets gave each planet an 'influence' or character, inspired by the personalities of the Greek and Roman gods and goddesses that they were named after. C.S. Lewis loved this symbolism and felt that it could help people to understand more about God. So he linked each Narnia story to one of the medieval planets, giving Aslan, the Jesus-figure, their positive qualities.

In *The Lion, the Witch and the Wardrobe*, Narnia is covered in snow, under the influence of Saturn (the cold planet) until Aslan arrives, kingly like Jupiter. Saturn rules again in *The Last Battle*, where there is war and death. Mars is the god of fighting and of trees, which both appear throughout *Prince Caspian*. *The Voyage of the Dawn Treader* is all about the golden sun, and *The Silver Chair* is about the moon with its watery, silvery properties. And so it goes on.

Listen to this conversation from *The Voyage of the Dawn Treader*:

'In our world,' said Eustace, 'a star is a huge ball of flaming gas.'

'Even in your world, my son, that is not what a star is but only what it is made of.' (VDT, ch. 14)

Do you like the idea of thinking of stars as not just 'flaming balls of gas'?

Extension activity

To find out more about Michael Ward's 'Narnia code', see www.planetnarnia.com.

Our Bible link: Matthew 13:3–9

Jesus often used parables (stories with a 'hidden' meaning) to help people to think more deeply about God and about their own lives. In this parable the different seeds are like people responding to God's love in different ways.

'A farmer went out to scatter seed in a field. While the farmer was scattering the seed, some of it fell along the road and was eaten by birds. Other seeds fell on thin, rocky ground and quickly started growing because the soil wasn't very deep. But when the sun came up, the plants were scorched and dried up, because they did not have enough roots. Some other seeds fell where thornbushes grew up and choked the plants. But a few seeds did fall on good ground where the plants produced a hundred or sixty or thirty times as much as was scattered. If you have ears, pay attention!'

Reflective corner

Props needed: Pictures of the galaxies

'Even in your world, my son, that is not what a star is but only what it is made of.' How can we explore new ways of seeing and doing things?

Worksheet: Medieval and modern views of the planets

Saturn

Jupiter

Mars

Sun

Venus

Mercury

Moon

Earth

Mars

Moon

Earth

Venus

Mercury

Sun

Jupiter

Saturn

Uranus

Neptune

Lesson plan: Beautiful world

Learning objectives

- To explore this key theme in the Narnia stories
- To understand how C.S. Lewis's worldview was influenced by the Bible
- To explore the concept of beauty and how we respond to it

Cross-curricular links

Art, Literacy, PSHE, Music

Starter

Show an image of the Rayonnant rose window in Notre Dame de Paris, easily found on the internet. In Gothic architecture, light was considered the most beautiful revelation of God. Has anyone visited this cathedral or seen any other stained-glass windows? Why do you think churches use stained glass? What does it add to a building?

Activity: What a wonderful world

Watch a video clip showing the beauty of the natural world—for example, from the BBC TV series *Planet Earth*.

C.S. Lewis was strongly influenced by his knowledge of the Bible when he wrote the Narnia stories. In *The Magician's Nephew*, the lion Aslan creates the new world of Narnia, bringing light out of darkness. Animals and people live together happily and two very ordinary human beings are put in charge. This is an imaginative retelling of the creation story in Genesis chapter 1. The following passage describes the moment of creation.

A voice had begun to sing... Then two wonders happened at the same moment. One was that the voice was suddenly joined by other voices; more voices than you could possibly count. They were in harmony with it, but far higher up the scale: cold, tingling, silvery voices. The second wonder was that the blackness overhead, all at once, was blazing with stars... If you had seen and heard it, as Digory did, you would have felt quite certain that it was the stars themselves which were singing, and that it was the First Voice, the deep one, which had made them appear and made them sing.

'Glory be!' said the Cabby. 'I'd ha' been a better man all my life if I'd known there were things like this.' (MN, ch. 8)

Some people say that 'beauty' is linked with being in balance and harmony with nature. As a class, discuss what the Cabby might have meant about 'being a better man' if he'd known such beauty existed. Do you agree that appreciating beautiful things could make you a 'better' person?

With a partner or in a group, describe the most beautiful thing you have ever seen. Was it from nature or something a person had made? Was it alive? Was it a person? How did it make you feel?

To take another angle, think about what makes someone (a celebrity, for example) beautiful. Is it simply about how they look or what they wear?

Activity: A heavenly sound

People in medieval times used to speak of the 'music of the spheres' —a harmony in the movement of the planets through the heavens. What might that music have sounded like? What instruments would you use to create it? Re-read the description of stars singing, in *The Magician's Nephew*, and try to make planet music in groups.

Alternatively, use some of Holst's *Planets* music and identify the character of each planet by listening to the music.

Our Bible link: Psalm 19:1–4

Psalm 19 was C.S. Lewis's favourite psalm.

The heavens keep telling the wonders of God,
and the skies declare what he has done.
Each day informs the following day;
each night announces to the next.
They don't speak a word,
and there is never the sound of a voice.
Yet their message reaches all the earth,
and it travels around the world.

Reflective corner

Props needed: A selection of beautiful pictures or objects

Whatever is true, whatever is noble, whatever is right, whatever is pure, whatever is lovely, whatever is admirable—if anything is excellent or praiseworthy—think about such things. (Philippians 4:8, NIV)

Think about some beautiful things.

Lesson plan: Spoiled world

Starter

Talk about a time when things went wrong. (This can be as light-hearted or serious as you feel is appropriate.) Encourage the class to share their own experiences. This could be done as a circle time activity.

Activity: Spoiled world

In the Narnia stories, C.S. Lewis seems to give two reasons why the world has been spoiled.

Reason 1: Conflict

The Narnia series is full of battles, evil rulers and power struggles. Even the 'good' characters frequently quarrel and fight. (See the 'Making choices' lesson plan for examples of this kind of conflict.)

Ask the children to brainstorm some ideas to try to resolve a situation where there is arguing and fighting. They could then use some of these ideas in a roleplay or series of freeze frames, or with puppets.

Reason 2: The 'dark side'

In *The Lion, the Witch and the Wardrobe*, Edmund meets the White Witch, who tempts him to betray his brother and sisters, giving him his favourite sweets and promising that he will be a king and rule Narnia with her.

Play the song 'Turkish Delight' by the David Crowder Band, with its refrain 'The more I have, the more I want…'. This can be found on the CD *Music Inspired By The Chronicles of Narnia* or on the internet.

Read the description of Edmund's meeting with the Witch:

Edmund felt much better as he began to sip the hot drink. It was something he had never tasted before, very sweet and foamy and creamy, and it warmed him right down to his toes.

'It is dull, Son of Adam, to drink without eating,' said the Queen presently. 'What would you like best to eat?'

'Turkish Delight, please, your Majesty,' said Edmund…

She said to him, 'Son of Adam, I should so much like to see your brother and your two sisters. Will you bring them to see me?'

'I'll try,' said Edmund, still looking at the empty box…

And he thought about Turkish Delight and about being a King ('And I wonder how Peter will like that?' he asked himself) and horrible ideas came into his head… (LWW, ch. 4 and 7)

What do the class find difficult to resist? It might not be food… it might be an activity or a habit. In *The Lion, the Witch and the Wardrobe*, Edmund was tempted by the Turkish Delight, but also by the promise of becoming a king. In our Bible passage below—a much older story—Eve, the first woman, was tempted by the tasty fruit, but also by the promise of becoming wise.

Invite the children to re-stage that moment in mime, with no talking but lots of gestures. Explain as follows:

'Get into pairs. One of you is the snake, the other is Eve. Imagine the snake is like a large Indian cobra, which can sit up on its coils, as high as a human. Perhaps it even has arms, like a lizard. Decide who's going to play which part. If you don't want to be Eve, you can be Adam, her husband—but we'll do the story just the same.

'Eve, imagine you're looking up at a fruit on the branches of a tree. You've never tasted it before, and someone has said it's bad for you. But oh... it looks so good... so juicy... so tasty...

'So you think about touching it, then draw back. But the snake points out how wonderful the fruit would taste, and how clever it will make you. You're persuaded. You reach out, touch it, pick it off the tree—and then you bite into it greedily. But the snake's looking really pleased with himself, and you wonder what's happened. Something has gone terribly wrong, but you don't know what it is.'

Practise the mime (using appropriate music if wished), and then ask some pairs to perform for everybody.

Extension activity

Read Matthew 4:1–4 and see how Jesus resisted temptation.

Our Bible link: Genesis 3:3–6

The snake was more cunning than any of the other wild animals that the Lord God had made. One day it came to the woman and asked, 'Did God tell you not to eat fruit from any tree in the garden?'

The woman answered, 'God said we could eat fruit from any tree in the garden, except the one in the middle. He told us not to eat fruit from that tree or even to touch it. If we do, we will die.'

'No, you won't!' the snake replied. 'God understands what will happen on the day you eat fruit from that tree. You will see what you have done, and you will know the difference between right and wrong, just as God does.'

The woman stared at the fruit. It looked beautiful and tasty. She wanted the wisdom that it would give her, and she ate some of the fruit.

Reflective corner

Props needed: A selection of current news stories (vetted for suitability of content)

Choose a news story that describes a bad situation. Write how you feel about it, or a prayer, on a Post-it™ note and stick the note to the story.

Lesson plan: Mended world

Starter

Talk about a time when something went wrong but was then sorted out and made better. (For example: finding a plaster for a cut knee, or a rubber for a mistake made when writing, or having a hug from a friend to say sorry.) Encourage the class to share their own experiences. Were they able to make things better by themselves or did someone else help them?

Activity: Coming to the rescue

In the Narnia stories, C.S. Lewis says that the world has been mended because of an amazing act of self-sacrifice and forgiveness.

Watch the sequence from the Walden Media film version where Aslan dies and comes back to life.

Because he has betrayed his brother and sisters, Edmund's life is forfeit to the White Witch, but Aslan steps in to save him and dies in his place, allowing himself to be killed on the Stone Table. Aslan returns to life, just as the 'magic deeper still' foretold—that 'when a willing victim who had committed no treachery was killed in a traitor's stead, the Table would crack and Death itself would start working backwards' (LWW, ch. 15). Aslan not only rescues Edmund but forgives him, so that Edmund is freed from feeling guilty, and encourages everyone else to forgive him too.

This is an imaginative retelling of Jesus' death on a cross to 'take away the sin of the world' (John 1:29). The Witch's followers mock Aslan—'Why, he's only a great cat after all! ... Puss, Puss! Poor Pussy... How many mice have you caught today, Cat?' (ch. 14)—just as people mocked Jesus in Luke 23:35–39:

While the crowd stood there watching Jesus, the soldiers gambled for his clothes. The leaders insulted him by saying, 'He saved others. Now he should save himself, if he really is God's chosen Messiah!'

The soldiers made fun of Jesus and brought him some wine. They said, 'If you are the king of the Jews, save yourself!'

Above him was a sign that said, 'This is the King of the Jews.'

One of the criminals hanging there also insulted Jesus by saying, 'Aren't you the Messiah? Save yourself and save us!'

As a class, discuss why Jesus stayed on the cross, taking the abuse from the people around, when he could have called on his Father to rescue him. Can you think of a situation when it would be the right choice to put up with something difficult, even though you could walk away and not go through with it?

Alternatively, think about how the story of Aslan's sacrifice can help us to understand why Christians attach such importance to the sacrifice of Jesus.

Activity: Putting it back together

Using broken items (without sharp edges) brought in from home, or torn-up art materials, work in groups to do junk modelling or make a collage or mosaic. See what beautiful things can be created out of spoiled and broken parts.

Our Bible link: Isaiah 61:2–4

The prophet Isaiah brings a message of hope and healing to the people of Israel.

The Lord has sent me
to comfort those who mourn,
especially in Jerusalem.
He sent me to give them flowers
in place of their sorrow,
olive oil in place of tears,
and joyous praise
in place of broken hearts.
They will be called
'Trees of Justice',
planted by the Lord
to honour his name.
Then they will rebuild cities
that have been in ruins
for many generations.

Reflective corner

Props needed: Photographs of the world, illustrating the ideas of 'spoiled' and 'mended' (for example, natural disasters, relief efforts and rebuilding)

Think of our world as spoiled… but mended. Is there anything we can do to mend it, by helping or forgiving?

Lesson plan:
Positive values

Learning objectives

- To be able to describe Aslan's key qualities
- To link these qualities with the descriptions of Jesus in the Bible
- To explore what C.S. Lewis is saying about positive values

Cross-curricular links

PSHE, Literacy, Drama, Art, Music

Starter

Families used to have mottos—key words about themselves and the things they felt were important. Write a motto that sums up what is most important to you, choosing three or four words such as: 'Family Friends Food Fun', or making a statement like the royal family's motto: 'Je me fie en Dieu'—'I trust in God'. You could design these words nicely and make a classroom collage with photos of each child.

Activity: Getting to know Aslan

C.S. Lewis uses the character of Aslan to embody positive values, drawing on the character of Jesus in the Bible. He wrote in a letter to some schoolchildren in Maryland in 1954:

Let us suppose *that there were a land like Narnia and that the Son of God, as He became a Man in our world, became a Lion there, and then imagine what would happen.*

The worksheet on pages 56–58 gives some examples of Aslan's 'positive values'. Looking at one example in each group, children should work to express that value through mime, art or music. (The extracts included from each book will give some visual prompts to help make the concept less abstract.) They should then perform or display their work to the rest of the class.

Extension activity

Aslan clearly represents positive values, but there are still some big questions to ask about some of the things he does or doesn't do:

- Throughout the series, characters spend a long time waiting for Aslan to come. In *The Lion, the Witch and the Wardrobe*, the White Witch has ruled Narnia for 100 years, making it always winter and never Christmas, before Aslan arrives and defeats her, ending the harsh winter. Why doesn't he come earlier?
- In *The Silver Chair*, King Caspian sails off to find Aslan because his son has been missing for years and he needs to know who should become king when he dies. Where was Aslan when the snake killed Caspian's wife? Why do bad things happen?
- Also in *The Silver Chair*, since Aslan knows everything that will happen, he must know that Jill will miss some of the signs he gives her. So why do you think he gives them to her? Why does he send Jill and Eustace to rescue Prince Rilian rather than just doing it himself?
- In *The Last Battle*, Aslan allows lies to be spread about him. He even allows himself to be impersonated, which leads to all sorts of bad things happening. He doesn't appear until the battle is over and the good side has been defeated. Why do good people suffer?

Suppose you could ask Aslan these questions. How do you think he might answer? Working with a partner, take turns to try to answer some of the questions as you think Aslan might do. Are there other questions you would want to ask about our world? This could lead into a class discussion time.

Reflective corner

Props needed: The family motto display (made in the Starter activity)

Think again about your most important values and how you can show people that these values are important to you.

Worksheet: Getting to know Aslan

1. Aslan is all-powerful

'I have swallowed up girls and boys, women and men, kings and emperors, cities and realms,' said the Lion. It didn't say this as if it were boasting, nor as if it were sorry, nor as if it were angry. It just said it. (SC, ch. 2)

Our Bible link: Revelation 1:8

The Lord God says, 'I am Alpha and Omega, the one who is and was and is coming. I am God All-Powerful.'

2. Aslan is fair

Aslan treats others fairly and encourages them to be fair, too. Sometimes this involves payback. Aslan chases Aravis across the desert and scratches her back. He later explains:

'The scratches on your back, tear for tear, throb for throb, blood for blood, were equal to the stripes laid on the back of your stepmother's slave because of the drugged sleep you cast upon her. You needed to know what it felt like.' (HHB, ch. 14)

Aslan also abides by his own rules. In *The Voyage of the Dawn Treader*, when Lucy speaks the spell to remove invisibility, Aslan appears and tells her that he has been there all along and that she has made him visible.

'Aslan!' said Lucy almost a little reproachfully. 'Don't make fun of me. As if anything I could do would make you visible!'

'It did,' said Aslan. 'Do you think I wouldn't obey my own rules?' (VDT, ch. 10)

'Don't condemn others, and God won't condemn you. God will be as hard on you as you are on others! He will treat you exactly as you treat them.'

3. Aslan is generous

In *The Silver Chair*, Aslan encourages Jill to trust him and drink from the stream he is guarding: 'If you're thirsty, you may drink.' (SC, ch. 2)

Our Bible link: John 7:37–38

On the last and most important day of the festival, Jesus stood up and shouted, 'If you are thirsty, come to me and drink! Have faith in me, and you will have life-giving water flowing from deep inside you, just as the Scriptures say.'

4. Aslan is self-sacrificing

In *The Lion, the Witch and the Wardrobe*, Aslan dies at the Witch's hands to save Edmund from being killed.

The Witch… gave a wild fierce laugh.
'The fool!' she cried. 'The fool has come. Bind him fast.'
Lucy and Susan held their breaths waiting for Aslan's roar and his spring upon his enemies. But it never came. (LWW, ch. 14)

Our Bible link: John 3:16

God loved the people of this world so much that he gave his only Son, so that everyone who has faith in him will have eternal life and never really die.

5. Aslan is merciful

In *The Lion, the Witch and the Wardrobe*, Edmund the traitor is forgiven, and in *The Last Battle* many unexpected people end up in Aslan's Country, some of whom never even knew him in their lifetimes.

Eustace even recognised one of those very Dwarfs who had helped to shoot the Horses. But he had no time to wonder about that sort of thing (and anyway it was no business of his). (LB, ch. 14)

Our Bible link: John 3:17

God did not send his Son into the world to condemn its people. He sent him to save them!

Lesson plan: Image and identity

Learning objectives

- To explore positive models of behaviour
- To identify specific positive behaviours to work on
- To recognise that we are all valuable and special

Cross-curricular links

PSHE, Literacy, Design and Technology

Starter

Take a couple of minutes to come up with as many positive adjectives as possible. Use a timer and work as a class or in pairs.

Activity: 'Just enough'

Aslan represents ultimate goodness in the Narnia stories, and the other characters look up to him as a role model.

Around an image of Aslan, write these key characteristics: all-powerful, fair, generous, self-sacrificing, merciful (see the previous lesson plan).

Who do you look up to? Who is your role model at home… at school… in the media?

What are the qualities needed to be a good role model? Using your list of positive adjectives, complete the Aslan picture, adding any other qualities that you think a role model should have.

Highlight any of those qualities that you think you have.

In *The Voyage of the Dawn Treader*, Lucy discovers a spell to make herself beautiful and is tempted to say it so that she can become more beautiful than her older sister, Susan. She manages to resist that temptation, but instead says the spell that lets her know what her friends think about her—which she then regrets. On the same island, the Dufflepuds have made themselves invisible because they thought they were ugly.

Listen to 'There's a place for us' by EMD, a song that talks about our identity: 'exactly who we are is just enough'.

Activity: New names

C.S. Lewis decided when he was a very small boy that he wanted people to call him 'Jack' instead of 'Clive' (his real name), and so, all his life, he was known as Jack. I wonder why he felt it was so important to give himself a new name.

At the end of *The Lion, the Witch and the Wardrobe*, Peter, Susan, Edmund and Lucy become kings and queens of Narnia. Each of them gains a positive adjective of their own:

- Peter 'the Magnificent'
- Susan 'the Gentle'
- Edmund 'the Just' (meaning 'fair')
- Lucy 'the Valiant' (meaning 'brave, courageous')

How would you like people to describe you? Design a crown with your chosen name on it: 'King/Queen … the …'

Alternatively, work in small groups to decide together what the best quality of each child is, and what he or she should be called. Some guidance may be needed to ensure that the discussion is constructive, but a positive name given by other children can prove very affirming.

Our Bible link: Matthew 16:17–18

Jesus gave one of his friends, Simon, a new name. This name was like a promise of the good things that Simon was going to do in the future—a name to live up to.

'Simon, son of Jonah, you are blessed! You didn't discover this on your own. It was shown to you by my Father in heaven. So I will call you Peter, which means "a rock". On this rock I will build my church, and death itself will not have any power over it.'

Reflective corner

Props needed: A mirror

How do you think you should behave to make the name you chose for yourself come true? Is there anything stopping you? Think of Edmund 'the Just', who let everyone down but was given a second chance and a new name.

Lesson plan:
Making choices

This material can be spread over two sessions, depending on the amount of time you wish to allow for the discussion questions.

Learning objectives

- To understand the importance of making good choices
- To explore some motivations for making bad choices
- To develop strategies for making the right choices

Cross-curricular links

PSHE, Literacy

Starter

Tell the children about a time when you made a good decision and a time when you made a bad decision. Can they explain to you why the good decision was good and the bad decision bad?

Activity: Getting it wrong, getting it right

The characters in the Narnia stories make lots of choices, some good and some bad. In the following scenes from the books, the class should try to predict which of the multiple-choice outcomes actually happened. You could read out the following questions and take a vote for each answer, or children could use the worksheet on the website, which gives the scenarios and the multiple-choice questions (but not the answers). The children should also be encouraged to think about what *should* have happened.

Scenario 1

In *The Magician's Nephew*, Digory and Polly are in a strange, magical world where anything could happen. They find a bell in a ruined palace, with an intriguing sign on it:

Make your choice, adventurous Stranger;
Strike the bell and bide the danger,
Or wonder, till it drives you mad,
What would have followed if you had.

'No fear!' said Polly. 'We don't want any danger.'
   'Oh but don't you see it's no good!' said Digory. 'We can't get out of it now. We shall always be wondering what would have happened if we had struck the bell.' (MN, ch. 4)

What happens next?
a) Polly persuades Digory to walk away from the bell.
b) Digory persuades Polly that there isn't really any danger.
c) Digory strikes the bell even though Polly tries to stop him.

Ask: Was this the right thing to do?

The answer: c) Digory strikes the bell... and wakes the evil sorceress Jadis. Wrong decision!

Discuss: Digory's curiosity gets the better of him. The sign 'dares' him to take the risk, and it sounds exciting. Talk about whether it is right or wrong to accept a dare.

Scenario 2

In *The Voyage of the Dawn Treader*, the children discover a pool that turns everything to gold—including the unfortunate man who dived into it, years ago.

'The King who owned this island,' said Caspian slowly, and his face flushed as he spoke, 'would soon be the richest of all the Kings of the world. I claim this land for ever as a Narnian possession. It shall be called Goldwater Island. And I bind all of you to secrecy. No one must know of this.' (VDT, ch. 8)

What happens next?
a) Edmund tells Caspian that he thinks this is a bad idea.
b) Edmund and Caspian start fighting about who the island belongs to.
c) Edmund and Caspian agree to split the profits between them.

Ask: Was this the right thing to do?

The answer: b) Edmund and Caspian start fighting. Fortunately Aslan appears and they come to their senses before any real harm is done. They name the island 'Deathwater Island' and leave.

Discuss: The temptation here is greed and the desire for money and power. Money is not a bad thing in itself, but what bad things might it lead to?

Scenario 3

In *Prince Caspian*, Lucy sees Aslan showing them the right path to take, but the others don't see Aslan and it doesn't look like the right way to go.

'The Lion,' said Lucy. 'Aslan himself. Didn't you see?' Her face had changed completely and her eyes shone. '... And he wanted us to go where he was—up there.'

'How do you know that was what he wanted?' asked Edmund.

'He—I—I just know,' said Lucy, 'by his face.' (PC, ch. 9)

What happens next?

a) Peter, Susan and Edmund tell Lucy she must be mistaken.
b) Peter and Susan tell Lucy she must be mistaken, but Edmund supports her.
c) All the children decide to go the way Aslan wants.
d) Lucy goes off by herself.

Ask: Was this the right thing to do?

The answer: b) Edmund chooses to believe Lucy, because he remembers a similar situation when Lucy found the way into Narnia and no one believed her.

Discuss: The children are tired and anxious and what Lucy is saying doesn't seem to make sense. It's hard to believe something we haven't seen for ourselves. Talk about Edmund and how he supports Lucy. Are there times when you have taken somebody's side or been their friend when they were on their own?

Scenario 4

In *The Silver Chair*, Jill Pole and Eustace Scrubb have suddenly arrived in Narnia. They are shocked to be there and are not thinking clearly.

They were at the very edge of a cliff.

Jill was one of those lucky people who have a good head for heights. ... She was rather annoyed with Scrubb for pulling her back—'just as if

I was a kid', she said—and she wrenched her hand out of his. When she saw how very white he had turned, she despised him.

'What's the matter?' she said. And to show that she was not afraid, she stood very near the edge indeed; in fact, a good deal nearer than even she liked. (SC, ch. 1)

What happens next?
a) Eustace reasons with Jill and she moves away from the edge.
b) Jill storms off in a temper.
c) Jill doesn't listen and, when Eustace tries to pull her back from the edge, he falls over himself.

Ask: Was this the right thing to do?

The answer: c) Eustace falls off the cliff. Aslan appears and saves Eustace by blowing him through the air all the way to Narnia, but Jill's actions get their adventure off to a very bad start.

Discuss: Jill feels annoyed with Eustace and reacts by trying to score points off him. How do we behave when someone annoys us?

Scenario 5

Aslan asks Jill where Eustace is, just after he has fallen off the cliff.

'He fell over the cliff,' said Jill, and added, 'Sir.' …
*   'How did he come to do that, Human Child?'*
*   'He was trying to stop me from falling, Sir.'*
*   'Why were you so near the edge, Human Child?' (SC, ch. 2)*

What happens next?
a) Jill admits that she was showing off.
b) Jill says that it was an accident.
c) Jill says that it was all Eustace's fault.

Ask: Was this the right thing to do?

The answer: a) Jill admits that it was her fault. This is one of Jill's good decisions.

Discuss: Jill is honest with Aslan and with herself. (She does find saying sorry to Eustace more difficult, though.) Talk about how admitting we have been wrong and apologising can clear the air.

Scenario 6

In *The Silver Chair*, a mysterious, beautiful lady advises the weary travellers to seek hospitality with the 'Gentle Giants' of Harfang.

Puddleglum didn't want them to go to Harfang at all. He said that he didn't know what a giant's idea of being 'gentle' might be, and that, anyway, Aslan's signs had said nothing about staying with giants, gentle or otherwise. The children, on the other hand, who were sick of wind and rain, and skinny fowl roasted over campfires, and hard, cold earth to sleep on, were absolutely dead set to visit the Gentle Giants. (SC, ch. 6)

What happens next?
a) Puddleglum persuades the children not to make the detour to Harfang.
b) Jill and Eustace insist that they all go to Harfang, and they end up in danger.
c) Jill and Eustace insist that they all go to Harfang, and the giants help them with their quest.

Ask: Was this the right thing to do?

The answer: b) They end up in danger. Puddleglum was right to want to concentrate on following Aslan's signs. The mysterious lady was trying to get them to forget their quest.

Discuss: The children are exhausted by their long journey, and the lady's promise that they will be warm and well fed at Harfang easily distracts them from where they are supposed to be going. When we are tired and don't want to do something, how can we keep our focus?

Our Bible link: John 14:6–7

Jesus described himself as being the direction for people's lives.

'I am the way, the truth, and the life! Without me, no one can go to the Father. If you had known me, you would have known the Father. But from now on, you do know him, and you have seen him.'

Reflective corner

Props needed: A map, picture of a road sign or compass

C.S. Lewis wrote: 'Every time you make a choice you are turning the central part of you, the part of you that chooses, into something a little different from what it was before' (*Mere Christianity*). What things help us to make the right choices in our lives? Why and how do they help us?

Lesson plan: Good friends

Starter

Ask the class to write down on Post-it™ notes what makes a good friend/brother/sister: 'A good friend does… A good friend doesn't…' Stick them up at the front of the class and read them out.

Activity: Me, me, me!

One bad thing that can happen in a school community is bullying. Let's hear about a school where the bullies were allowed to do what they liked and the teachers didn't stop them.

Listen to the start of *The Silver Chair* using this three-minute audio file: www.collinseducation.com/resources/SilverChair.MP3.

That community had gone wrong because people were only thinking about what they wanted and not about each other.

Let's look now at Uncle Andrew (Mr Ketterley) in *The Magician's Nephew*, who has just locked Digory and Polly in his study to get them to take part in a dangerous experiment:

'Please, Mr Ketterley,' said Polly. 'It's nearly my dinner time and I've got to go home. Will you let us out, please?'

'Not just yet,' said Uncle Andrew. 'This is too good an opportunity to miss. I wanted two children. You see, I'm in the middle of a great experiment.' …

'My earlier experiments were all failures. I tried them on guinea-pigs. Some of them only died. Some exploded like little bombs—'

'It was a jolly cruel thing to do,' said Digory, who had once had a guinea-pig of his own.

'How you do keep on getting off the point!' said Uncle Andrew. 'That's what the creatures were there for. I'd bought them myself.' (MN, ch. 1 and 2)

Do you think Digory is 'getting off the point'?

What adjectives would you use to describe Uncle Andrew? (Selfish, uncaring, cruel…)

Can you see his point of view, though?

Let's take another example: the ape Shift in *The Last Battle*.

Shift had one friend and neighbour who was a donkey called Puzzle. At least they both said they were friends, but from the way things went on you might have thought Puzzle was more like Shift's servant than his friend. He did all the work… Puzzle never complained, because he knew that Shift was far cleverer than himself and he thought it was very kind of Shift to be friends with him at all. (LB, ch. 1)

Do you think Shift is being kind?

With a partner, roleplay a conversation where one person is asking the other person to do something that isn't fair or that the second person doesn't think is right (for example, doing their homework for them, breaking a school rule, lying…). What should the second person say?

Activity: Looking out for each other

What is friendship really all about? Talk about the importance of being friendly to people and helping them even if you are not 'best friends'.

Make a simple friendship band out of a strip of coloured paper and write on it something that you will make more of an effort to do (for example: 'I will always say hello to my classmates'; 'I will smile more at people'; 'I will listen better when my friend is upset'; 'I will talk to the person who is on their own'). These bands could then be tied together and hung up in the classroom as a reminder.

Play 'The call' by Regina Spektor (from the Walden Media film version of *Prince Caspian*), which speaks about always being there for each other.

Our Bible link: Ecclesiastes 4:9-10, 12

This passage from the Old Testament suggests that friendship isn't just about having fun together.

You are better off having a friend than being all alone... If you fall, your friend can help you up. But if you fall without having a friend nearby, you are really in trouble... Someone might be able to beat up one of you, but not both of you. As the saying goes, 'A rope made from three strands of cord is hard to break.'

Reflective corner

Props needed: The friendship bands made in the activity above, or paper chains or plaited cords

What are the things that join us together? How can we 'join together' to make our school community a better place?

Lesson plan:
Building a better world

Learning objectives

- To understand the importance of working together
- To explore what a good community should look like
- To articulate the challenges of building a good community

Cross-curricular links

PSHE, Citizenship, Literacy, Design and Technology

Starter

Brainstorm some ideas for change within the class or wider school community. How could we make our school more friendly/more welcoming, and so on? Keep the discussion positive!

Activity: Bad leaders

This is how Digory describes his Uncle Andrew: 'He thinks he can do anything he likes to get anything he wants' (MN, ch. 2). When people like this are in charge, C.S. Lewis says, things go badly wrong in society. In *Prince Caspian*, the young Caspian starts to realise this:

As a little boy he had often wondered why he disliked his aunt, Queen Prunaprismia; he now saw that it was because she disliked him. He also began to see that Narnia was an unhappy country. The taxes were high and the laws were stern and Miraz was a cruel man. (PC, ch. 5)

In *The Magician's Nephew*, the city of Charn is ruined because Jadis has destroyed it:

This place was at least as quiet as the Wood between the Worlds. But it was a different kind of quietness. The silence of the Wood had been rich and warm... and full of life: this was a dead, cold, empty silence. (MN, ch. 4)

With a partner, build something out of Lego™.

Different pairs of children should be given different instructions:

- Both children try to cooperate with their partner and listen to what the other person wants.
- Both children try to do it their way and do not listen to the other person's suggestions. (Keep a close eye on these groups in case they get out of hand!)
- One child does it their way and the other child just lets them.

After five minutes, bring the class back together and compare notes. How do different pairs feel about the experience? Are they happy with the results?

Activity: Good leaders

In *The Magician's Nephew*, Aslan makes Frank and Helen king and queen of the newly created world of Narnia. He tells them:

'You shall rule and name all these creatures, and do justice among them, and protect them from their enemies when enemies arise.' (MN, ch. 11)

Being king or queen of Narnia is a responsible job. How should Frank and Helen behave? Write a list of five things that they should do as good leaders, and five things that they should not do.

What laws should they pass? Write their manifesto (a public declaration of principles and intentions). The article http://geoffmcdonald.com/the-manifesto-manifesto gives guidelines on how to do this. It is important to use strong, positive language.

Can the class create its own manifesto? Once it is written, read it out proudly! (This may link in with the starter activity, and could provide an opportunity to reinforce class rules and expected behaviours.)

Our Bible link: Genesis 11:1-9

Is it a good thing for people to be able to do 'anything they want'? In this ancient story God decides that it is not.

At first everyone spoke the same language, but after some of them moved from the east and settled in Babylonia, they said: 'Let's build a city with a tower that reaches to the sky! We'll use hard bricks and tar instead of stone and mortar. We'll become famous, and we won't be scattered all over the world.'

But when the Lord came down to look at the city and the tower, he said: 'These people are working together because they all speak the same language. This is just the beginning. Soon they will be able to do anything they want. Come on! Let's go down and confuse them by making them speak different languages—then they won't be able to understand each other.'

So the people had to stop building the city, because the Lord confused their language and scattered them all over the earth. That's how the city of Babel got its name.

Reflective corner

Props needed: A badge of office such as a prefect's badge or teacher ID card

Think about: Who is responsible for making our school community the best place it can be? If things go wrong, who should put them right? What could you do?

Drama workshop

These ideas could be used in one or two stand-alone sessions or incorporated into any of the preceding lesson plans.

Learning objectives

- To roleplay through movement, music and imagination
- To express emotions through a range of different media
- To explore and analyse emotions through a range of different media

Cross-curricular links

Drama, Music, PSHE, Literacy

Activities

Ice breaker

The White Witch is turning people to stone. The children should 'freeze' and then come back to life. One adult could be the White Witch, saying, 'Freeze!' and another adult could be Aslan, saying, 'Be alive again!'

Express those feelings

Use body language to show:

- Edmund feeling that his older brother Peter is getting at him (resentful).
- Mr Tumnus regretting the choices he's made (devastated).

- Lucy when no one believes that she has found the land of Narnia (upset/defiant).
- Peter about to kill the wolf Maugrim (terrified).
- The Witch when she realises that winter is over (furious).
- Aslan going to meet the Witch, knowing that she will kill him (sad).

Awe and wonder

Using 'The wardrobe' (track 3 of the official soundtrack to the Walden Media film) as background music, mime coming through the wardrobe and finding a snowy land beyond. How can you show that it is very cold? How can you show that you are in a forest?

Arriving in Narnia

Roleplay some of the following characters. (Children should add their own thoughts and exclamations.)

- Lucy, going through the back of the wardrobe (LWW, ch. 1): 'This wardrobe goes back a long way! Why is it so cold? What are these rough, prickly things? Oooooooooh…'
- Peter, Susan, Edmund and Lucy, being pulled from the station platform (PC, ch. 1): 'Stop tugging at me!' 'I'm not doing anything—you're pulling me!' 'Something strange is happening…' 'Quick, everyone—hold hands!'
- Lucy and Edmund, being drawn into the picture of the *Dawn Treader* (VDT, ch. 1): 'The picture's moving!' 'The waves are going up and down!' 'How wonderful! We're in Narnia again!'
- Eustace, being drawn into the picture of the *Dawn Treader*: 'I'm in the water! Help! Get me out of this terrible place at once!'
- Jill and Eustace, escaping from the school bullies (SC, ch. 1): 'Quick! We've got to get away from them!' 'I hope the door in the wall is unlocked… but it's never unlocked…' 'It *is* unlocked!' 'Oh my goodness, where is this?'

Poetry performance

Learn one of these short poems from the books and practise reciting it. Highlight or underline sections of text to add one area of emphasis per line, and plan one simple gesture per line to bring it alive.

Make your choice, adventurous Stranger;
Strike the bell and bide the danger,
Or wonder, till it drives you mad,
What would have followed if you had. (MN, ch. 4)

- Tone of voice: thrilling, warning, tempting

Wrong will be right, when Aslan comes in sight,
At the sound of his roar, sorrows will be no more,
When he bares his teeth, winter meets its death,
And when he shakes his mane, we shall have spring again. (LWW, ch. 8)

- Tone of voice: confident, hopeful, triumphant

Where sky and water meet,
Where the waves grow sweet,
Doubt not, Reepicheep,
To find all you seek,
There is the utter East. (VDT, ch. 2)

- Tone of voice: wondering, joyful, encouraging

Dilemmas

Act out the scenarios from the 'Making choices' lesson plan (see pages 63–68), or roleplay them using your own words.

Movie moments

Watch, enjoy and evaluate the trailers for the first three Walden Media films, readily available on the internet.

Getting into character

Organise a Narnian dress-up day.

Assemblies

Christmas: 'Winter passed'

Monday: Whole-school collective worship

> Aim: To talk about Christmas as a time of joy and hope

Ask who has read the book or seen the film of *The Lion, the Witch and the Wardrobe*.

Show the clip from the Walden Media DVD where the faun Tumnus explains to Lucy that in Narnia it is always winter but never Christmas (Scene 4, from 18:50 to 19:25).

- Ask the children how they would feel if they were waiting for Christmas but it never came. What would it be like?
- Imagine Christmas with no presents and no fun with friends and family. The Witch forbids people to celebrate. What else does the Witch take away? Christmas represents hope for the future, but the Witch wants the future to be exactly the same as the present—cold and bleak and with nothing to look forward to. She takes away the changing seasons. Imagine the trees being bare all year round.

Show the clip of the snow beginning to melt (Scene 13, from 1:13:20 to 1:14:10).

- When Aslan returns, there is spring... new life... and people are free to be glad and hopeful. Christians believe that the birth of Jesus at Christmas time was God's way of bringing hope into our world.

Reflection/prayer

In a quiet moment, think about a time when you've been in a difficult situation and couldn't see it ever changing. Perhaps you are in that situation now. Think of spring following winter and the new beginnings that are possible. If you want to, you can say your own prayer, asking God to help you and give you hope.

Follow-up ideas for 'Thought for the Day' through the week

Tuesday (in classrooms)

Read Psalm 27, which ends, 'Trust the Lord! Be brave and strong and trust the Lord.' Who do you turn to for help?

Wednesday (in Key Stage groups)

Discuss the following sayings about hope:

Hope is that thing with feathers that perches in the soul and sings the tune without the words and never stops… at all.
EMILY DICKINSON

The miserable have no other medicine
But only hope.
WILLIAM SHAKESPEARE, *MEASURE FOR MEASURE*

Hope is patience with the lamp lit. ´
TERTULLIAN

Learn from yesterday, live for today, hope for tomorrow.
ALBERT EINSTEIN

Thursday (in classrooms)

What can we do to bring hope to other people at Christmas time?

Friday (whole school)

Feature an organisation that brings hope at Christmas time, such as Viva (www.viva.org), which provides Christmas parties for children at risk, or Shelter (www.shelter.org.uk), which helps the homeless.

Easter: 'Guilt forgiven'

Monday: Whole-school collective worship

Aim: To talk about the significance of Easter in Christian belief

Ask who has read the book or seen the film of *The Lion, the Witch and the Wardrobe*.

Show the clip from the Walden Media DVD where Edmund meets the White Witch (Scene 6, from 29:20 to 32:10).

- Ask the children if they think that Edmund knows the Witch is bad. If he does know, why is he doing as she says? What does she promise him?
- Edmund cannot resist Turkish Delight—and the promise of being a prince! What are the things that you just can't resist?
- Edmund's decision causes a lot of trouble. He lies to his brother and sisters and is found out; he becomes the White Witch's prisoner and is badly treated; and, worst of all, the White Witch has a claim on his life, even when he has been rescued from her.

Show the clip of the White Witch arriving at Aslan's camp to claim Edmund's life (Scene 14, from 1:28:15 to 1:30:05).

- In the story, Aslan dies in Edmund's place and comes back to life. Christians believe that Jesus died instead of us on Good Friday and came back to life on Easter Sunday, bringing new hope for everyone.

Reflection/prayer

In a quiet moment, think about a time when you did something wrong. What were the consequences? Did someone forgive you? If you want to, you can say your own prayer, asking God to help you to do the right thing in future.

Follow-up ideas for 'Thought for the Day' through the week

Tuesday (in classrooms)

Read chapters 23 and 24 of Luke's Gospel, which describe Jesus' death on the cross and his resurrection. Talk about how Jesus' friends, both the women at the tomb and the disciples on the road to Emmaus, were given new hope after having none.

Wednesday (in Key Stage groups)

Edmund is a changed and nicer person after Aslan rescues him and dies for him. In the Bible, a man called Saul went around attacking the new Christians until he realised that this was wrong. Then he travelled all over the Roman Empire, telling people about Jesus. Read the account of Saul's change of mind, in Acts 9:1–19. Do we believe that big changes are possible in our own lives?

Thursday (in classrooms)

What change would we like to see in our community? How can we make it happen?

Friday (whole school)

Focus on an initiative—community, national or international—that works to bring healing and restoration to painful situations.

Plot summaries

The Lion, the Witch and the Wardrobe was the first story to be written, and *The Magician's Nephew* and *The Horse and His Boy* were written later as 'flashbacks'. However, the stories are presented in chronological order here to make the overall storyline of the series easier to follow.

The Magician's Nephew (1955)

- London, 1900: Digory Kirke and Polly Plummer are sent to the Wood between the Worlds by Digory's Uncle Andrew, who is using them as human guinea pigs to test out the magic rings he has made.
- The wood is full of pools like the one they arrived through, and the children decide to explore one of the other pools.
- They find themselves in the ruined world of Charn. Inside the palace, in a room full of statues of ancient kings and queens, Digory strikes a bell that awakens the last of the statues, a beautiful queen, from an enchanted sleep. The queen, Jadis, had killed every living creature in Charn by speaking a 'Deplorable Word', and is now looking for a new world to conquer.
- Digory and Polly try to get away, but Jadis clings to them as they return to their world. In England she wreaks havoc until the children grab her and put on their magic rings to take her out of their world, accidentally dragging Uncle Andrew, Frank the cab driver, and Frank's horse with them.
- In the Wood between the Worlds, they jump into a pool leading to a world that hasn't yet been created.
- A lion, Aslan, appears and sings the new world—Narnia—and all its creatures into existence. Jadis, hating the lion, escapes.
- Aslan commands Digory to make amends for bringing the evil Witch into this new world by going to a garden far away and bringing back an apple from the tree he finds there.
- Jadis has got there first and eaten one of the magic apples to make herself immortal, but her face is now 'deadly white'. She tempts Digory to take the apple to heal his dying mother, but Digory follows Aslan's orders and returns to Narnia with the apple, which is then planted in the ground.
- A new tree grows up, which Aslan says will protect Narnia from the Witch for many years. Aslan tells Digory that the stolen

apple would have healed his mother physically, but both she
and he would have lived to regret it.

- With Aslan's permission, Digory takes an apple from the new
  tree to heal his mother. Aslan sends Digory, Polly and Uncle
  Andrew back to England, and Frank and his wife, Helen (whom
  Aslan brings from England), become Narnia's first king and
  queen.
- The apple cures Digory's mother, and he plants the core,
  together with the rings, in the garden. The wood from this tree
  is later made into a wardrobe.

The Lion, the Witch and the Wardrobe (1950)

- 1940: Peter, Susan, Edmund and Lucy Pevensie are evacuated
  from London during World War II to escape the Blitz. They
  go to live with Professor Digory Kirke in a big house in the
  countryside.
- Lucy goes into a wardrobe during a game of hide-and-seek and
  discovers that it leads to a magical world—Narnia. She makes
  friends with Mr Tumnus the faun, who is under orders to betray
  her to the White Witch (Jadis) but decides to protect her.
- The others do not believe Lucy's story about Narnia, but soon
  Edmund finds his way in through the wardrobe. He meets
  the White Witch, who wants him to bring his siblings to her.
  She bribes him with Turkish Delight and promises that he will
  rule over the others. Edmund keeps his visit to Narnia secret,
  making Lucy out to be a liar.
- Eventually all four of the children enter Narnia together. They
  meet Mr and Mrs Beaver, who tell them the prophecy that the
  White Witch's power will end when two Sons of Adam and
  two Daughters of Eve sit on the four thrones at Cair Paravel.
  They also speak of the true king of Narnia, the lion Aslan, who
  is now returning after many years' absence.

- Edmund sneaks away to the White Witch. The other children and the Beavers, realising that they are in danger, race to meet Aslan at the Stone Table with the Witch in pursuit. The snow melts as the White Witch's power starts to fade.
- The children join Aslan and his army and rescue Edmund, but the Witch claims that Edmund's life is forfeit to her since he is a traitor. After a private conversation with Aslan, she renounces her claim.
- That night, Aslan leaves the camp secretly but is followed by Lucy and Susan. He has agreed to give his own life for Edmund's. The Witch ties Aslan to the Stone Table and kills him, but the following morning Aslan comes back to life.
- With Lucy and Susan, Aslan rushes to the Witch's castle to breathe on the statues of the creatures that the Witch had turned to stone, bringing them back to life. The Witch is defeated in battle and the children become kings and queens of Narnia.
- Several years later, they stumble back through the wardrobe and arrive in England as children again.

The Horse and His Boy (1954)

- During the 'Golden Age', when Peter, Susan, Edmund and Lucy are kings and queens in Narnia, Shasta runs away from home after hearing his fisherman father planning to sell him to a Calormene nobleman.
- He escapes with the nobleman's horse Bree, who comes from Narnia and can talk, but has kept this ability a secret.
- They join forces with Aravis, a Calormene girl from a noble family, and her talking horse Hwin. Aravis is running away to Narnia to avoid an arranged marriage. Aravis and Shasta don't get on very well but realise that their chances of escape are better if they all stay together.
- Their route lies through Tashbaan, the Calormene capital city. A group of visiting Narnians mistake Shasta for Corin, prince of

Archenland, and he has to go with them, leaving the others to fend for themselves.

- The Narnians are afraid that Queen Susan will be forced to marry the Tisroc's son, Prince Rabadash, and Shasta overhears their plans to leave Tashbaan secretly. The real Prince Corin returns and helps Shasta to escape.
- Meanwhile, Aravis's friend Lasaraleen helps Aravis to escape through the Tisroc's palace. Hiding, they overhear the Tisroc and Rabadash planning to invade Archenland and Narnia.
- Outside Tashbaan, Aravis, Shasta and the horses regroup and set out across the desert. A lion (Aslan) chases them and they outrun Rabadash's army.
- Shasta arrives in Archenland in time to warn King Lune of the attack, and the Calormenes are defeated.
- King Lune recognises Shasta as Cor, the long-lost identical twin of Prince Corin and heir to the throne. Aravis and Cor eventually marry.

Prince Caspian (1951)

- Peter, Susan, Edmund and Lucy are called by magic from a station platform back into Narnia—to discover that it is now hundreds of years after they left. Their castle, Cair Paravel, is in ruins.
- They rescue a dwarf, Trumpkin, from soldiers who are about to drown him. Trumpkin tells the children that the Telmarines now rule Narnia and the talking animals and dwarves are in hiding.
- King Miraz is in charge, having usurped the throne by killing his brother. Miraz's nephew Caspian is the rightful heir.
- When the queen has a son of her own, Caspian's life is in danger. Warned by his tutor Doctor Cornelius, he escapes and seeks out the Old Narnians.
- They gather for a council at midnight, but Doctor Cornelius arrives to warn them that Miraz and his army are on their way.

They take refuge at Aslan's How (the ancient site of the Stone Table).
- The Telmarines follow and attack them. Seeing no alternative, Caspian and his followers decide to use Queen Susan's horn, which Doctor Cornelius had given to him, to summon help. (This is what has brought the Pevensies back into Narnia.)
- After a long and eventful journey, Trumpkin and the children arrive at Aslan's How. Peter challenges Miraz to single combat. When Miraz falls, his own lords stab him to death.
- The Telmarines surrender and Aslan gives them the choice of staying in Narnia under Caspian or returning to Earth, their original home, through a magic door. The children return to their world and find themselves back on the station platform.

The Voyage of the Dawn Treader (1952)

- Edmund and Lucy, together with their unpleasant cousin Eustace Scrubb, are drawn into Narnia through a picture of a ship at sea. Caspian, now king of Narnia, rescues them out of the sea on to his ship, the Dawn Treader.
- Caspian is on a quest to find seven of his father's friends, whom his uncle Miraz had sent on a dangerous voyage. Lucy and Edmund are delighted to be back in Narnia, but Eustace complains bitterly. The talking mouse Reepicheep is also on board, hoping to find Aslan's Country in the 'utter East'.
- In the Lone Islands, Caspian, Lucy, Edmund, Eustace and Reepicheep are captured by a slave trader, but they are rescued by the first lost lord, Lord Bern, who had married and settled there. Caspian reclaims the islands for Narnia and replaces Gumpas, the corrupt governor, with Bern.
- After a storm, they land on another island to repair the ship. Eustace goes inland to avoid helping with the work. He discovers a dying dragon and its hoard and takes some of the treasure, including a golden bracelet. As he sleeps, he is

transformed into a dragon. The experience teaches him how selfish he has been, and he is then turned back into a boy by Aslan. The bracelet belonged to Lord Octesian.

- They survive an attack by a sea dragon and land on Deathwater Island, where they find a pool of water that turns everything to gold—including, at some time in the past, the missing Lord Restimar.

- At the next island, invisible creatures force Lucy to enter a magician's house to find the spell to make them visible again. Aslan appears to Lucy, who is tempted to try some of the spells she reads in the magician's book. The creatures are made visible, as is the magician himself, who is not at all the evil being that they had described.

- The travellers rescue Lord Rhoop from the Dark Island where (bad) dreams come true, and Aslan's albatross destroys the island.

- At Ramandu's Island they find the three remaining lords deep in an enchanted sleep. Ramandu, a star in human form, tells them that the only way to wake the lords is to sail to the edge of the world and leave one person behind there.

- The *Dawn Treader* sails on until the water becomes so shallow that the ship can go no further. Caspian is tempted to go to the world's end, but Aslan reminds him of his duties as king and his promise to Ramandu's beautiful daughter that he will return.

- Lucy, Edmund, Eustace and Reepicheep travel on through a sea of lilies until they reach a wall of water that reaches the sky. Fulfilling Ramandu's condition, Reepicheep paddles his coracle up the waterfall. Aslan sends the children home.

The Silver Chair (1953)

- Eustace and his classmate Jill Pole are being chased by bullies at their horrible boarding school, Experiment House. Eustace suggests asking for Aslan's help, and they open a door in the school wall, hoping to escape that way. To their astonishment, it leads to the top of a high mountain in another world.

- Jill shows off by going too close to the edge of a cliff, and Eustace, trying to pull her back, falls over the edge. Aslan appears and saves Eustace by blowing him through the air to Narnia.
- Aslan tells Jill that she and Eustace need to find Prince Rilian, Caspian's son, who disappeared more than ten years before, and gives her four signs to remember and follow. The final sign is that, at a crucial moment, they will be asked to do something in Aslan's name.
- Aslan then blows Jill to Narnia. She arrives a few moments after Eustace—just as a frail, elderly king sails away on a voyage. They realise, too late, that this was Caspian (much older, as Narnian time has passed more swiftly) and that they have failed the first sign, which was that Eustace should speak to an old friend.
- Glimfeather and the other talking owls explain that Prince Rilian disappeared while searching for the green snake that killed his mother. It is likely that the snake is one and the same as a beautiful woman in green who appeared to Rilian around that time.
- Jill and Eustace begin to travel north, following the signs, accompanied by the Marsh-wiggle Puddleglum, and pass safely through giants' territory.
- Crossing a huge, ancient bridge, they meet the Lady of the Green Kirtle and a silent knight in black armour. The Lady encourages them to go to Harfang, the castle of the 'Gentle Giants', who will welcome them for their Autumn Feast. Once she has described the food and comforts they will find there, Jill and Eustace can think of nothing else.
- The Gentle Giants do indeed welcome them, but in the morning the children look out of a window and see the words 'Under Me' on the tableland below. This is Aslan's third sign.
- They plan to escape, made more determined by their discovery that the giants are planning to eat them at the Autumn Feast.

Chased by the giants, they hide in a hole and fall down a slope into Underland.

- Strange earthmen take them across the Sunless Sea to the city ruled by the Lady of the Green Kirtle. The Lady is away, but her companion (the black knight) welcomes them. He seems friendly, but there is something strange about him. He explains that every night he is tied to a silver chair by the Lady's orders, for if he is released he will turn into a green snake and kill everyone in sight.
- However, when the knight is tied down, he begs to be released 'in the name of Aslan', and Eustace, Jill and Puddleglum obey, as this is the final sign. Once released, he announces that he is Rilian, whom the Lady—or Green Witch—has kept under a spell, planning to invade Narnia and set him on the throne as a puppet-king.
- The Lady returns and tries to bewitch them, but Puddleglum stamps out her magical fire and breaks the spell. She transforms herself into a green snake, and Rilian kills his mother's murderer.
- They escape from Underland as the flood set in motion by the Witch's death starts to destroy the city. The earthmen joyfully return to their home deep in the earth.
- Rilian arrives at Cair Paravel to meet his father as he returns home, and they are reunited just before Caspian dies. Aslan takes Jill and Eustace back to the mountain and then sends them home.

The Last Battle (1956)

- It is the 'last days' of Narnia. Roonwit the centaur warns King Tirian that strange, evil things are happening.
- A cunning ape named Shift has persuaded his friend Puzzle, a donkey, to dress in a lion's skin and pretend to be Aslan. The Narnians are tricked into thinking that Aslan is angry with them and is going to punish them.

- Shift orders the Narnians to work for the Calormenes and to cut down trees to sell, killing the spirits who live within them. The money will be paid into 'Aslan's' treasury, held by Shift.
- King Tirian and his friend, Jewel the Unicorn, realise that everyone is being deceived when they hear Shift telling the Narnians that Aslan and the Calormene god Tash are one and the same.
- When Tirian challenges Shift, the Calormenes take him prisoner. He calls on Aslan for help and sees a vision of Digory, Polly, Peter, Edmund, Lucy, Jill and Eustace, though he does not know who they are. Jill and Eustace arrive in Narnia, release the king and rescue Jewel and Puzzle.
- Tirian and his friends fight the Calormenes, and all the Narnians are killed.
- Tirian ends up in the stable where the false Aslan was kept, to discover that it contains Digory, Polly, Peter, Edmund, Lucy, Jill and Eustace in a beautiful landscape. Susan is not with them. The god Tash swallows Shift and the evil Calormene leader Rishda Tarkaan, but then Peter orders Tash to leave.
- Aslan appears and the fate of all the people and animals is decided as they go through an enormous door. Those who have been loyal to Aslan join him in Aslan's Country. Those who have opposed or deserted him vanish.
- Narnia is brought to an end, with dragons eating the vegetation and Father Time calling down the stars into the sea, which rises to cover the land. The sun expands and draws in the moon, and then Father Time puts it out.
- Peter closes the door, and Aslan leads them to his country—the 'real' Narnia. In a beautiful garden they meet many old friends.
- The children see their parents arriving from England. Aslan explains that all of them have died in a train crash, but that this is just the beginning of the true story, 'which goes on for ever'.

Barnabas RE Days: exploring Christianity creatively

Our Barnabas RE Days explore themes such as 'Whose world?', 'What's so special about the Bible?' and 'Who am I?' through biblical and personal stories, contemporary life illustrations and shared experience, addressing many PSHE/Citizenship objectives. The sessions use different creative arts, such as storytelling, music, dance, mime, drama, creative writing or drawing, according to the particular skills of the team member undertaking your booking.

The timetable, class groupings and themes are completely flexible and can be organised between you and the Barnabas team to suit your school's needs. A full-day visit costs just £275, of which £50 is placed down as a non-returnable deposit when booking. For more information, contact the Barnabas Team Administrator on 01865 319704 or email barnabas@brf.org.uk.

What's so special about Narnia?

Have you heard about the 'Narnia' Barnabas RE Day? Using a mix of games, storytelling and drama, a member of our Barnabas team can give your pupils a taste of Narnia, leading them together through some key scenes in the stories by C.S. Lewis, linking RE, Literacy and PSHE. Many children are used to 'doing' Easter (or Christmas) once a year in school, but our Barnabas RE Day aims to enhance understanding of the first Easter by drawing parallels with what happened at the Stone Table in Narnia.

Why do this? Because we believe in the imaginative life of children, and that some truths about the Christian faith are best discovered, explored and remembered through stories. That's how Jesus taught the crowds of his own time, using parables to plant the seeds of new ideas in the human memory as teaching illustrations, then leaving them as unexplained mysteries to flourish and grow in the imagination. Many of C.S. Lewis's stories have the same effect: they can present an apparently stale idea in a startling new light, giving a fresh perception of ancient truths.

A free copy of *Teaching Narnia* is provided to all booking schools, and free support materials for teachers are available on our website at www.barnabasinschools.org.uk/extra-resources/, alongside a training programme for teachers. We hope your school will be interested.